Was

Poetry by

Elizabeth Ouzts

2022

Copyright © 2022 Read or Green Books
Albuquerque, New Mexico

Cover Art by Elizabeth Ouzts
Interior photographs by David Ouzts & Elizabeth Ouzts

All rights reserved. No portion of this publication may be reproduced or transmitted in any form without prior permission of **Elizabeth Ouzts** unless such copying is expressly permitted by Federal copyright law. Addresses, questions, comments send to: Read or Green Books: marissa@ReadorGreenBooks.com.

Visit our websites:
www.ReadorGreenBooks.com
www.ShaneManier.com

FIRST EDITION
ISBN: 978-1-73781-637-9
Produced in the United States of America

Dedicated to Jason and Mad.

I love you more than words.

Was

Contents

Foreword

I have written since I was a child and love words in all their forms. From poems and novels to letters and crossword puzzles, the power of words and those who wield them leaves me in awe. After years of writing very little, I have come back to words, or perhaps they have come back to me. They help me find my voice and the power in my own words that I left somewhere in my twenties.

This collection is 30 plus years in the making. It includes poems written in college, poems dusted off and reworked, and poems that showed up just last week. They are the sights, sounds, and memories of a free-range childhood in South Carolina and a life spent loving flowers, photographs, books, and family.

I hope somewhere among them you find delight.

"In this century, and moment, of mania,
tell me a story.

Make it a story of great distances, and starlight.

The name of the story will be Time,
but you must not pronounce its name.

Tell me a story of deep delight."

Robert Penn Warren, Audubon: A Vision, 1969

WAS

The house that once stood
In a clearing
Between two fields of corn
Now sits
On the brink of falling –
Becoming earth again

A tin roof
Of gray and rust
Dented by summers of hail
Struggles to hold up collapsing walls

Splintered porch rails
Lean forward and back
Threatening to twist apart
If a slight breeze pushes past

Windows
Shattered in cobweb shapes
Hang brown with dirt on dirt
From too little rain
And long unplanted fields

Inside
On a moldy pine floor
Chipped glasses, bowls, and plates
Lie
Under twenty or more years of dust

While black spiders weave transparent shrouds

RESOLUTION, FROM THE LATIN "RESOLVERE"

Before we made this
a new year's attempt
to force ourselves to be better
do more
stop that
start this
it meant to release
to loosen
to give over and
let things go

This year I will let go of self-hate,
people who are no longer friends,
fears that no not serve me
loosen the tight red threads
of anxiety
that cut off my circulation
like a string on my finger
reminding me that everything
will never be okay

I will unwind the knot
that sits a millimeter in front of my heart
causing beats to skip
pressing on my lungs
so no breath
is ever a deep cleansing one

I will slacken the noose
that will snap my neck
every time
she's sad for too long,
in the bathroom with razors,
asleep for days
all the things
that will rock the chair
from beneath my feet

MIDDLING INVISIBLE
with thanks to Cara and Makenna

She was,

she later learned

from the dictionary of obscure sorrows,

middling invisible,

not quite

not there

but blissfully hovering

on the periphery

opaque in her averageness

coming to mind

only rarely

when the winds and words stilled

and the world held its breath

SLIP AWAY

There is something I remember
each morning
as I wake
That slips away as I
tell myself I won't forget

The perfect phrase
drifts away
a dust mote in a ray of sun
captured by a tiny demon
bent on collecting all those things
on the tip of my brain

memory that will not hold
just out of reach

words on scraps of paper
brilliant at their writing
but now strange strings of random words
offering no clues to whatever the hell I thought was worth
writing down
what the hell could I have been thinking

words written in the dark
almost illegible in the daylight
"the thing that breaks your heart"
scrawled on a receipt
and I have no idea
if that's the answer to a question
or the beginning of the next poem

ASHES

Walking through the ruins
Again in my mind
Two years after the arson

I can see the chimney
Surrounded by a pile of house –
Ashes and charred wood still smoking

Can still hear siren, water,
The hiss and crackle
Of dying embers
Dying chairs and books and baby pictures

But now
What bothers me
Is that I can't remember the smell

Then – when it was all fresh
And I was in shock
I thought that when all else faded
I would never lose that smell –
The stench
Of everything I owned

previously published in: The Poetry Peddler, (1989)

FOR ONCE, THEN NOTHING

I read Robert Frost
Then walk
Through his New England
And find a well of stone and mortar
That may have inspired him
Once

And then, like him before
I kneel
And lean far enough
To see my face
Framed by reflected walls
And am surprised to see
A flicker of something white
Then I wonder
Is it quartz or truth
Or a bottle cap irreverently thrown
In a convenient spot?

I try not to think about it
But there is something there – I think
Or at least for a moment
For once, then nothing…

WINTER, ALASKA 1964

He does not know what the hell happened
But he is outside
Freezing cold in the midday sun
Such as it is
On a winter's day in Alaska

The girls
One pigtailed
One bobbed
Bundled against the elements
Squint and smile

Their
shadows
stretching
Impossibly
tall
Draping
the
house
And
the
bike
That
will
not
move
until
the
thaw

WINTER WANDERINGS

The rare snow in Jackson's Mill
Brought everyone out
To see the crisp white clouds
That settled
Early Thursday morning.

Bundles of striped and solid wool
Not worn since the big storm ten years ago
Slowly walked and slid and fell
Down the trail that leads into the woods behind the house
Then stood
And tried to look through a tangle of scuppernong vines–
A frozen lattice
Nailed together by thin icicles

Then turned toward home
When the cold became too much
To see a bluebird's nest
Shining like a cut glass bowl.

The rare snow in Jackson's Mill
Made each snowball stored behind frozen peas
A treasured crystal ball
That told of winter wonderings
And seventeen inches of snow
In early March.

WEEKENDS AT GRANDMOTHER'S

Weekends at Grandmother's
Rowesville, SC
Nowhere on the map

We battled the witchy pecan
with sticks and rocks

Rode the giant propane tank,
an elephant or horse or car

Ran with the goats
Swinging orange glass citronella lanterns

Our pool
A rusted wheelbarrow

The only danger
An electric fence
We'd all grabbed

And like memory
Could not let go

CEDAR CHEST, FOR FRANK RAYMOND

The cedar chest Granddaddy made
Four months before he died
Sits in his workshop
Gathering dust
Waiting for me to bring it home

But there is not enough room in my house
Or my life
Not yet
For a reminder of what I lost
when a broken vessel took him out of reach
It is too soon for the absence of tears
when I think of the smooth wood
Sanded, outside and in,
By hands rough from years at the lumber yard

Time has not taken me far enough from January
That I can bear the smell of cedar and varnish
Or flannel shirts and aftershave
So for now the chest sits
And patiently waits
For me to bring it home
And fill it with as much love
As he put into it

ONE MILE UNDER TENNESSEE

In a cave
in Tennessee
the guide
turns off
the pink and green lights
used to "highlight the natural beauty"
of the rock

And for the first time
I saw
not seeing
the complete nothingness
of darkness

And though I knew
my hand
was two inches from my face
there was
for a moment
doubt that it or I existed

SPRING IN GIVERNY, 1890, MONET

Green flecks merge with oranges and blues
For a meadow

Colors collide
Gently
To become tree, sky, earth

Hints of yellow and white
Still visible
In a dimly lit room

Thousands of snowflakes
Creating eternal spring

MORNING GLORY

The bed is twice as big this morning
As I lie in twisted sheets
While you – up for hours –
Begin to grope for pots and a cookie sheet
The fifth attempt at a breakfast in bed

FALLING OUT OF A CANOE ON GREEN RIVER

First
The pain of the rocks,
The garble of voices
Then,
The bubbling of water
Above, below – within
And now
There are only the dream women
With their huge woven baskets
Filled with orange daylilies
And leather-leaf fern
Floating by
Taking away my headache
Singing Sunday school songs
Then disappearing
As opal balls
Bounce and roll across silver grass
With the sound of crystal clinking
And a finger tracking the rim
Of a half empty glass
And I close my eyes
then open them
Realizing that what I see
Is the same–
Open or closed
Completely white rocks, voices, water
Outside and in…

GENTLE LEAVES

Behind my mother's house
A mimosa
With gentle leaves
That fold
From the touch
Of butterfly wings
Has been spattered
With thousands of blossoms–
          white makeup brushes
                    dipped in strawberry pink powder

                    And in its shade
          Queen Anne's lace
Sways slowly

Marking the hours of our childhood
Spent
Making potions from honeysuckle
One
drop
at
a
time

Chains of clover blooms
Delicate and sweet
Offerings for the fairies
My sister and I knew
Lived just beyond
Our imagination's reach

QUIET

An aloe grows in the window sill

And at night

The shadow of an oak

Presses itself against the blinds

Gently

A mother pressing her face

To the softness of her child –

Then reaches out to the red clay pot

And whispers –

Something –

That only those with chlorophyll

Decipher

BILLINGSLEY IN APRIL

She waits

staring through the green wall
then counting the tiles

checking texts every two seconds
for someone to stop this

supply the fix
fade the scars

make her perfect girl
perfectly whole

DRIVING OFF HIGHWAY 25 N CROSSING THE CENTER LINE TO FOLLOW THE SUN

The drive home
From the one that I now call my mother's
To the one I call my own
Is an easy drive with only two real turns –
One right, one left
And curve after curve that hypnotize

And on a June day
With the heat of six o'clock
Moving through the windshield
I begin to rock slightly – side to side
As I watch green fields of corn
And other plants whose names I can't recall from botany
Slide past
Right
Left
Right

Then I notice the sun
Draped by a sheet of cream haze
With rays visible
Like the pictures in my old Children's Pictorial Bible
With Jesus standing white-robed, palms upturned
Basking in the sunbeams of God

And for a moment I expect to see a miracle, a pot of gold, a mythical bird
But instead there is a Black man
Riding a blue tractor across his field
Slowly turning over
Warmed red clay

Miles and fields pass

And without calling attention to itself
The haze breaks into thin clouds
Then the sun rolls off a cloud shelf
Disappearing for a moment
Turning the clouds to glowing orange sherbet
And suddenly swings down into view
Hanging as if by static electricity
Over the road
Now paved with diamond dust, silver shavings, and thousands of tiny mirrors

On the path into the sun
There is no center line
On the highway north
The edge skims my left
Then right
Then disappears from the mirror
As I drive toward the sun
Off the road
And into shrouded telephone pole of kudzu

90% HUMIDITY

After rain

On a June day

Steam rises –

Even from the grass

And dark legs

under a pale cotton dress

Stick
Slightly

When uncrossed

I LEAVE DOORS OPEN

I leave doors open
on the off chance
that opportunity
wants to come in
without knocking

I leave windows up
for fairies
and hope
and desperation

I leave the flue open
for obvious reasons

But drawers must be closed
for order
for appearances
to keep the secrets in
and eyes out

ONE DOOR

When one door closes
Another door opens
But sometimes it's the door
to an empty elevator shaft
Pitch black
Echoing empty
One step and you're gone

Or a louvered door
Squeaky hinges
Jamming at every attempt
To close
So you just give up

Or a Dutch door
The top locked
So you have to duck under
Careful not to bump your head

When one door closes
Maybe don't look for other open doors
Find a window
So you can see what's next

OOPS

The poem was whole again
The typing done
The glue dried clear
And the tape wasn't really noticeable on the back
It was folded and ready to be mailed

Until William startled me –
Wrapped his arms around my waist
From behind
And whispered,
"That's nice,
But wouldn't it flow more smoothly if…"

And I dropped it
And could only watch
As it flew into fragments on the floor
An allusion slid under the couch
With the dust bunnies and potato chips
A well-conceived image
Was wedged under the bookcase
And a yardstick was needed to pry it loose

ON THE VERGE OF NIGHT

On the verge of night
I sit on the porch
and sweat
hoping words will flow out
and drop onto this page
the fan cools
but not enough
for thoughts to condense

I stretch right, left
Relax my shoulders
searching for a comfortable stance
a moon salutation
gone slightly awry

My favorite blue pen
Held tight
Starts a word
But meanders into a flower
Then a five-pointed star
and rows of triangles

I focus on my breath
intent in, words out
pen to paper in a series of positions
each meant to give rise
to a meaningful thought
a goddess, a crescent, a mountain

CHRISTMAS LIGHTS

Christmas lights on the screen porch
still up in June
compete with fireflies
fewer
and further
between
still magical and miraculous

You shine like those lights
Steady and strong
unfaltering
set to come on at 7
and go off at midnight
Artificial but dependable
until the power goes out
a summer storm
blowing trees onto transformers
then you go dark
useless glass baubles on a line

I'm the flickering insects' pale flash
creamy yellow
lasting just minutes
after the sun goes down
and the temperature drops
flashing a signal to the universe
see me
see me
but eclipsed by you
until the thunder rages
and the ozone snaps
the connection

SHADE

The shadow drips
from the water oak
and is snagged
by the chain link fence
        water drops caught
        on the threads
        of a spider's web

CICADAS

Cicada screams
saw into the night
thunder rumbles
and rumbles
across a gray green black sky
then an eerie silence
since they know
what is coming
and when it is safe

that same quiet
after the call
driving to the ER
knowing I will be met with the howl
and crackling of ozone
as my child's mind
veers off course
battered by wind and stinging rain

CROWS

The crows who do not belong here
Jolt me out of a reverie of sun and shore
With loud fucking caws
And awaken sleeping cicadas
Who hum and thrum their song for two minutes
Then return to their dreams of flight and sex

I do not live here but in my marrow I belong as did my mother and hers before her
I have come here to write
and find a voice silent for too long
To play at painting
and discover hidden shades at my core

The words have to be perfect
But the colors can dance and swirl and drip
Across the page
Sensual, filled with hate, blissed out and gin drunk

ISLE OF PALMS

She steps onto the porch
Then stands
Leaning to the sea –
Her palms pressed on the thick, low railing
As a storm-cooled wind
Jangles
Thin yellow shells strung into chimes

Walking down the stairs
Toward the dunes
Of swaying sea oats
She pushes her blonding hair
Back from her face
And watches the sun come home

She brings her freckled fingers
To her lips–
Covering a waking yawn–
Then tastes the back of her hand
To find her salt
And the sea's
Indistinguishable

Standing
Alone
She writes her name in the sand
Watching the steam
Rise from the ocean
After a heavy rain

GREEN KNEES

Two children sitting
In freshly cut grass
Piled into an awkward nest
Wanting to become birds
When they grow up
Noses running, knees green from play

June bugs flying in circles
One leg tied to a string
Lightning bugs flickering
In a Duke's mayonnaise jar
An endless supply of living toys
Losing their lives to childhood games

Girls with pig tails, ponytails, braids
Skipping through puddles
Of warm mud
Feet orange and legs spattered
Shaking the lowest branches of the dogwood
Making it rain all over again

A white ice cream truck
Jingling down Dead Fall Road
Calling the young
Cold drips of banana sugar water
Hit scorching pavement
And disappear in seconds

Two children sitting
In freshly cut grass
Living before fears of death and life
Breathing the wisteria and honeysuckle
Knees green from play

Previously published in: Of Earth and Sky, (2021)

MIXED MEDIA

White swirls and delicate marks
Poppy red and bold blue strokes
Sunshine yellow, ever present
Layered color over black lines

Uncertainty and fear of failure
Each added color bringing confidence and focus
Strength combined with subtlety
Things I was not aware I could do

Summer, flowers, and movement
A chaos of color, shape, and texture
Merged into a happy dance
Fluttering leaves and birds across the page

SUNDAY

Sitting alone in the library
In late afternoon
There is only the even hum
Of the air conditioner
And the occasional thunk
Of a wasp
Meeting itself on the glass walls
As a slow rain
Muffles
The lives within

THE MOUNTAIN

The mountain
is velvet black tonight
A freshly erased blackboard
Matte black wrought iron
Not from a recent fire, unforgiving and swift
But from heavy rains
fist-sized drops
warm and smelling of earth
that turned the pale green
of katydids
so rich and luscious
that it is pitch from here

And I am at peace
my heart
love soaked
dark and flooded
with memories
of a first date
an observatory
and a view into the past
one kiss
then two paths
in an expanding universe

SUMMER STORM

The sparrows and bluebird stop
Leaving silence
Until thunder rattles the screen door
And the good crystal
Threatens to shuffle out of the China cabinet

The succulent smell of rain on pine
Lets you forget - for a moment - thoughts of fire
While the fake pearls hanging on the mirror's edge
Beat on the glass
Anxious fingers tapping

Hail
Bounces off the storm windows
Marbles dropped on a glass table
While sweetgum leaves wrap the house
In a wet cocoon.

As charges smash into the earth
With a force you can smell

SNAKE

"i am accused of tending to the past…"
-Lucille Clifton, Quilting: Poems 1987-1990

I am accused of tending to the past
As if I had anything to do
with all that treachery and hate

As if the hot coiled misery
wrapped around my heart was my own doing

As if I could have stopped it
squeezing the joy out of me
and slithering back through the dirt
under the gate
out into the world

2 GIRLS AND 4 PINES

Decades ago
In Alaska or Oregon
Two young women I do not know
Stand
In the middle of a field
Unaware of the photographer
Rapt in conversation
And bundled against the first chill of fall

On the left
Head bowed
She listens intently to her friend,
Smiling and animated,
A sensible skirt and knee socks

"And then we went to the movies
And after drove up to the Burger Barn
And he laughed so hard
Soda came out his nose!

We're going again next weekend
If you want to come too
It'll be fun
I promise."

Trying to convince her of the fun to be had
If she'll just give it a chance
If she'll not study all weekend

She will not go
Though she says maybe
There's more to her than dates and movies
Bare legged and braids
And a coat of flowers
Orange, red and yellow
Even in black and white

FREE FALL

It is not so much that I am afraid of heights
Not the height itself
But the prospect of falling from heights
The urge
To jump

I know one day
Maybe it will happen
On the tenth floor of a condo
Overlooking the Atlantic
Where in seconds I could push myself
Over a thin rail – a thin line –
And be with the gulls –
And then god?

Or maybe it will be when a Ferris wheel
At a county fair
Stops on the top and swings
Back
and
Forth

It will not be that I want to
I will have to

Previously published in: Echo (1990)

OVERGROWN

Confusions of roots
And tangles of weeds
Slowly pry the doors
Of a gutted Oldsmobile
Open
And grip the steering wheel –
The hands of a fifteen-year-old
Driving home from the DMV

And at dawn
Morning glories
Shine from headlight sockets

Previously published in Metamorphosis Publications' Visions Anthology, (1989)

WORDS

We form words

then wind our stories around spines

we twist our fears into knots

necklaces impossible to untangle

our hopes into spider webs

strong and fragile

an oxymoron

of thread

NOW

The sound that moves me to sleep
Is no longer my mother's off-key "que sera, sera"
Or Daddy's snoring
That annoyed me at midnight
But frightened me when it stopped

Now

Whatever will be is becoming - happening
And I fall asleep to Vivaldi's Four Seasons
With the volume turned up enough
So "Spring" drowns
Maggie and Don Smith downstairs
Yelling about who had no business checking on who
And the trills of "Winter"
Outdo the ambulance on Tenth Avenue

DAILY DELIGHTS OR TRAUMA THERAPY HOMEWORK

To heal the wounds
I am finding daily delights
listing them
one
by
one
in a notebook
shared only with my therapist

the list
is a poem
of good and great things
small and large that moor me here
and move the anchor out of the deep

a cat on a leash
snow on a Monday
Christmas lights in March
late blooming azaleas
toddler sized collards

things that at once surprise
and slam me into the now
that is still good
still worth staying

I AM

I am biscuits and grits
        screened porches and the screech
                of cicadas

I am swing sets
        sandboxes
                a playhouse with lights

I am sweet tea
        Sunday school
                water skiing at the lake

I am turkey and dressing and
        oyster roasts
                driveways 2 miles long

I am pine trees, dogwoods,
        queen Anne's lace
                beside an old dirt road

I am cars on blocks
        trees growing through tractors
                barns collapsing on themselves

I am kudzu, Sunday lunch at Bebe's
        Two meats, 4 veggies
                perfect yeast rolls

I am Raymond's grocery,
        a giant wheel of cheese
                a walk-in freezer

I am 100-pound bags of rice,
  medicated salt licks,
    a loaded gun

I am deer season, turkey season
  quail season, dove season
    shotguns and rifles

I am blue tick hounds
  blue crabs
    Uncle Johnnie's "camp" on the marsh

I am pluff mud
  sandy towels
    porpoises and shrimp boats

I am Flower's Seafood
  the Sea Cow
    Botany Bay

I am vacations to one house
  beachfront, big porch
    family

I am highway 25
  from college
    to home

A lineage of kindness
  a childhood
    as comfortable as a cotton dress

Knowing I mattered
  and was loved
    as much as I love those things long past

Acknowledgements

Thank you to Jason who loves me and supports me in every endeavor and makes me laugh with the world's best (worst) puns. Thank you to Maddie who inspires me daily and tells the world's next best puns. I love you both to infinity plus infinity.

Thank you to my parents and sister who always have faith in me and read my first poems when I was little.

Thank you to Shane Manier for her inspiration, coaching, and huge heart. Thank you to Marissa Prada for her wisdom and guidance in getting this book to press.

Thank you to Kimberley Reynolds for 18 years of friendship and sage advice and to Marianne Huebner for helping me rediscover delight in the world. Thank you to Cara Perry-Tracy and Makenna Tracy for being my first readers and asking amazing questions.

Thank you to Dr. William Aarnes and Dr. Gilbert Allen for teaching me what it is to be a poet. Thank you to my second-grade teacher, Mrs. Goodman, who made me memorize the poems of Robert Frost and Carl Sandburg.

Finally, I am so very thankful for all my family and friends who have cheered me on and shared my excitement about this book.

About the Author

Elizabeth Ouzts is an escapee from the world of corporate finance who is learning to trust herself as a poet, artist, and person.

She's been lucky enough learn from and become friends with amazing poets and artists who have supported and encouraged her as she finds her voice and style and decides what's next.

A volunteer for social justice, advocate for ending period poverty, and avid data geek, Elizabeth lives and works in Charlotte, NC, with her husband, teenager, and 2 nutty cats.

When she's not working, writing or painting, Elizabeth can be found reading, gardening, or sitting on her back porch.

Instagram: @feouzts1122
Facebook: www.facebook.com/eouzts
Website: www.elizabethouzts.com